Unbroken

Unbroken

A DREAM FOR MY SISTER

Sunny Lambe

To order additional copies of this book, contact:
Xlibris
UK TFN: 0800 0148620 (Toll Free inside the UK)
UK Local: (02) 0369 56328 (+44 20 3695 6328 from outside the UK)
www.Xlibrispublishing.co.uk
Orders@Xlibrispublishing.co.uk
835489

Contents

In memory of my sister,
Rashidat Iyabo Fodesho (nee Lambe)

Preface

The aim of this autobiographical account is to share personal life experiences with readers in the hope that it might help readers to understand that whatever your situation and circumstances in life, they are only temporary and will surely change for the better. Your future is right in your hands, but it depends on what you make of it and if you rise to the challenges along the way, wherever they may come from. Despite the challenges and late start to my education, I now have numerous degrees and qualifications; I am an Oxford University alumnus. The journey of a thousand miles always start with the first single step.

I would like to acknowledge everyone who has inspired me to great heights in life. Among them are my dad; my grandpa; my godmothers, Chief Mrs Omotola Oyediran and Mrs Alice Akinde; and my godfather, Professor Olukayode Oyediran. Most important, my father, Jacob Folorunsho Ayobandele Lambe, and grandfather, Adebayo Ogunkunle Ajadi Ogundiya. They showed me the value of integrity, determination, aspiration, compassion, self-dignity, and hard work. Also, my wife, Jean, who has been and continues to be my source of inspiration, strength, and support, despite the challenges.

Chapter 1

CHILDHOOD AND SIBLINGS

Sunny and his two sisters, Toyin and Iyabo, were the three surviving children of their parents before their marriage came to an abrupt end just after the birth of Toyin, the youngest sibling. Their parents were living in their family house in Ibadan, western Nigeria. Sunny's parents started very well together and were very much in love with each other as a young couple, since they both grew up in the same neighbourhood. After running away from working on his dad's farmland to look for a future outside farming, Sunny's dad, Jacob, started very well in life as a bricklayer. Following the end of his bricklaying apprenticeship programme, he started work with the Public Works Department of what was then the Western Government of Nigeria, earning a reasonable monthly wage to live on and look after his wife and children. Life was good for the family. However, things were about to change with irreparable consequences for the family.

On this fateful day, something terrible happened to Sunny's dad. He woke up that morning and bid good morning to his wife. As he came out of the bedsit room they shared as a couple and stepped into the communal lounge area, he suddenly realized he felt itching in his both eyes. He kept rubbing his eyes, thinking any particles causing the discomfort might come out. Sadly, without success. He was quickly rushed to the local Oniyanrin General Hospital for medical examination. The specialists tried their utmost to save his sight, but to no avail. It was eventually decided that perhaps they could replace both his eyes with optical implants from a cat or other animal, with the forewarning that his sight would never be same again. This was a time when optical medical advancement was in the embryonic stage.

Grandpa Adebayo, patriarch of the family, ordered that Jacob should be returned home for traditional treatment. This went on for several months and then years without restoring his sight. Everything that could be sold or pawned was disposed of in the hope of Jacob regaining his sight. Sadly, their efforts were in vain.

Meanwhile, the family started disintegrating. Sunny's mum, Mariam, moved to her parents' house for support since Jacob, the main breadwinner, was now housebound, and his savings exhausted in search of a cure. Could anyone blame Sunny's mum for making this drastic decision to relocate to her family home with her three children?

Sunny's dad was left to the mercy of his family for daily sustenance. There was no social security for the unemployed or a disabled person as a safety net in the country. This was the beginning of life struggles for both Sunny and his sister Iyabo.

Mariam's relocation to her family home was meant to be a temporary measure to seek some support for herself and her three children, Sunny and his two sisters. To become an *adelemosu*, a woman moving back into her parents' family home, was never encouraged in the Ibadan Yoruba tradition. It was believed that 'a woman shall leave mother and father to form and nurture her own new family' and live happily ever after. Perhaps this only happens in Disney movies. However, in those days, it was a taboo for a permanent separation of couples or breaking of marriages.

Sadly, adelemosu later escalated into the complete disintegration of the whole Lambe family, with disastrous consequences, especially for Sunny and his older sister, Iyabo. To compound the already challenging situation, Toyin, their youngest sister, developed a medical complication which put additional pressure on their mother and made life unbearable for her and her children, while Jacob was still struggling to regain his sight.

In order to relieve Mariam of some of the unbearable stress of single parenthood, with the youngest barely a year old, Grandpa Adebayo called a family meeting, as was customary. It was decided to have Jacob Lambe's older sister, Iya Eleko, foster Iyabo and Sunny's future put on hold. This was the point at which the children began to be separate.

As time went on, Mariam was not coping well with having to care for Sunny and Toyin without social benefits and adequate family support. Her husband was still being cared for by his own family, and nobody was sure whether it was temporary or permanent. Because Mariam seemed overwhelmed by the responsibilities of looking after her children on her own and had begun a new relationship, another family meeting was held to see whether relieving Mariam of Sunny's care might ease the pressure a bit more.

At this point, Jacob miraculously regained his sight. He had converted from atheism to Cherubim and Seraphim Christianity through an introduction by a family friend and workmate. He became an evangelist, playing the *shekere*, a traditional Yoruba musical instrument, and singing in his angelic voice.

The Lambe siblings' separation and family breakup was now complete: Toyin lived with their mother; Iyabo with her aunt, their dad's older sister; and Sunny moving in with his dad, a single parent. The latter posed another problem. Jacob promised that he would devote all his life and time to Sunny's upkeep, so he was allowed temporary custody of Sunny to relieve Marian of the mounting stress, which now included a baby from her new relationship.

And that is how Sunny, at just over three years old, ended up living with his single-parent dad.

Sunny lived happily with his dad in Ibadan for a few years, until Jacob decided to relocate to another state within Western Nigeria. It was not long before stories that Sunny's dad was not coping well with Sunny's care reached the grandfather and family patriarch. It was felt that Sunny might not have a stable life as his dad remained single, and that Jacob might need family help with Sunny's upbringing. (Jacob remained a single man until his peaceful passing in March 2012.)

So it was time for the extended family to hatch a plan to rescue Sunny from his unmarried dad. In those days, any single man or woman of marriageable age was regarded as irresponsible. Therefore, Sunny's dad, a man devoting all his life and love to his son, was regarded as irresponsible and his son as in need of rescue. Therefore, Sunny's aunt decided to rescue her nephew from his dad and put him in the care of the granddad who lived in a farmhouse in Ayegun Village. ironically, where Sunny's dad had met his mother, and the same farmhouse Jacob ran away from as a young man because he did not want to live in the village.

Chapter 2

LIFE IN A VILLAGE

It is often said that every disappointment comes with some blessings in disguise. Though happy with his single-parent dad, Sunny, like any child cut off from the rest of his extended family for so long, was excited at the prospect of a reunion, especially with the siblings whom he probably could not recognise if he saw them.

When he arrived at his grandpa's village, the old man was yet to return from his farms. Grandpa Adebayo had inherited a couple of plantations of cocoa, coffee, plantain, banana, and other food crops from his dad. Since none of his older children, including Sunny's dad, wanted to get their hands dirty on the farm, Grandpa Adebayo saw the future in Sunny helping to manage the farm and hoped to secure those family treasures in his hands.

Grandpa Adebayo told Sunny stories about the history and traditions of the family, their culture, heritage, and military prowess. He told Sunny how Ibadan people always bear their father's first name, which is why Sunny was also to bear his dad's first name and Lambe as his surname. Otherwise, it should have been Fijabi. Sunny learned that his granddad came from a line of kings, and his great-great-great-granddad was King

Fijabi the First (Oba Olubadan), who signed the protectorate treaty with the British in 1897 after the Kiriji War, following the civil war in Yorubaland.

Grandpa Adebayo would take Sunny to all his traditional meetings as a village chief, Baale Ayegun, a chieftaincy title he refused numerous times before Sunny moved in with him. Sunny and Grandpa Adebayo became so close and inseparable that no one would have ever known they were grandson and grandfather.

During this time, Grandad Adebayo had two wives living with him on the farmstead—a younger wife betrothed to him after Jacob's mum died, and the senior wife, who lived in the main Ibadan family house, whilst the most senior wife lived alone in the city family home.

However, there was one negative consequence of Sunny's relocation to his grandfather's house: He could not start his primary school education at the right age in September of that year, contrary to the promise made to Sunny's dad before he was lured away to his grandad. Sunny spent almost seven years with his granddad in Ayegun Village, nearing the age of thirteen with still no formal education.

Meanwhile, Sunny's dad had returned to Ibadan from Araro in Ogun state. He was still unmarried but had a stable job as a civil servant in the construction sector. So another plan was hatched, this time to lure Sunny away from his grandfather, who had gotten used to having him around and was reluctant to let him go. Sunny had become his indispensable soulmate and village baale's errand boy. In his quest to keep Sunny with him, he promised to put Sunny in a local village primary school, a promise later broken, to the disappointment of Sunny's dad.

Chapter 3

RITES OF PASSAGE

In the Yoruba African culture, the significance of grandparent patriarchal influences cannot be overemphasised. It is probably similar in other cultures around the world. Following Sunny's birth at the hospital, they returned to the family home Mum and Dad shared with the extended family in Nalende. Sunny's naming was followed by face marking with a tribal mark. Tribal marks are given to newly born babies within a few days or weeks of their birth, before it is too late to indicate which family or tribe he or she is from. The marks are used for identification and recognition to enable that child to trace his or her way home in case the child gets lost, stolen, kidnapped, or sold into slavery. So it was essential to name Sunny on the eighth day and decide on when to give him his family tribal mark, 'Gombo'.

On presenting Sunny (Sunday, born on Sunday) to Pa Adebayo, his grandpa by the biological parents, for naming as tradition demands, all sorts of names poured from extended family members—uncles, aunties, Muslims, Christians, traditional religion worshippers, and so on. But the final decision on the matter of first names and whether to get a tribal mark came from the grandfather as the patriarch of the family. So, Pa Adebayo, holding Sunny in his hands, said, 'This one will continue to bear the name Sunday the gods gave him from heaven. I have no power to change it. He will also avoid the knives of *oloola*, the traditional mark on his face.' He continued, 'The only thing we can do to Sunday is to circumcise him as soon as he is old enough to bear the ordeal.' It was reported there were grumblings from the extended family members during the ceremony expressed in traditional ways—breaking and sharing kola nuts, honey, sugar, water, salt, and necessary ingredients used for such occasion in the Yoruba, Ibadan, African cultural naming ceremony.

There was hardly any child born into the family who escaped having the traditional mark planted on both cheeks. But no one could argue with the patriarch of the family. Grandpa's decision was final. And this was how Sunny escaped having the tribal mark on his face and kept his name, Sunny (Sunday).

Chapter 4

SAVING SUNNY LAMBE

Rescue Plan 3

Following his dad's return to Ibadan town, it was time to hatch plan to rescue Sunny—rescue plan, round three. Sunny's aunt felt guilty that she was responsible for luring him away from his dad, who could have put him in school. So she decided to put the third rescue plan in action. It was similar to the first two, on paper. Of course, there were some modifications, including the fact that Sunny's dad was well involved.

Prior to the execution of the new rescue, news came that Sunny's mum was just a few miles away, visiting her mother, with whom Granddad was in regular contact. So a visit was arranged for Sunny to visit his mum at his grandma's in Onibonnla Village. This would be the first reunion between Sunny and his mother, at the age of about twelve going on thirteen. On arriving in his grandma's village, Sunny was met by two women, probably in their early thirties, sitting in the passage. Sunny greeted them in the traditional Yoruba way of greeting elders by prostrating in full as a sign of respect. Unknown to Sunny, one of the women was his mother.

And his mother did not recognize her son. So Sunny went straight to his grandmother, whom he had met through his grandfather a couple of times in the past.

When he reached the main living room area, he saw more guests, including the grandmother. The grandmother, Iya Alakara, started crying while holding on to Sunny as if she would never let him go. Everyone was surprised by Iya-Agba's cry. When she was able to compose herself, she asked Sunny's mum to join her and her other guests in the living room. She asked Sunny, 'Do you know who this woman is?' When Sunny responded with an emphatic no, Mama Agba turned to Sunny's mum and asked the same question. She also said no. Grandma Iya Alakara sobbed profusely this time. She embraced both Sunny and his mum and said, 'Gbenjo, that is your son. Sunday, that is your mother.' Sunny and his mother did not meet again for another seven years after Sunny relocated to his dad.

On Sunny's return to Grandpa following the reunion with his mum, rescue mission round 3 was put in action.

Grandpa Adebayo was told that Sunny was only going to visit his dad for a couple of days. It had been more than seven years since they saw each other. So Grandpa Adebayo agreed to the visit, not knowing it was the last time Sunny would ever work on his plantation, or that it would take another several years for them to be reunited. In fact, Grandpa moved back to the city a few years after Sunny left.

Saving Sunny Lambe round 3 was successfully accomplished!

Chapter 5

RESCUE MISSION 4

When Sunny was about ten years old, he and his dad were reunited. But Sunny had still not been enrolled in any formal education or training programme. He was, however, enrolled with a private tutor his dad was paying to help Sunny catch up with his education. Instead of being in an education, employment, or training (NEET) programme, Sunny was seen hanging around some undesirable elements. Although a good boy, these individuals were perceived as bad influences that could easily lure Sunny into criminal activities.

So it was felt that perhaps yet another rescue mission was appropriate and necessary. Access and contacts between parents, siblings, and extended families would not pose any problems because all family members now lived within the same Ibadan city.

Prior to reunion with his dad, Sunny's aunt had been registered at a local primary school when the dad threatened to come and take Sunny back. The only person left out of the conversations was Sunny himself. However, the good thing that would come out of moving back to Auntie's house was the opportunity for Sunny and his sister Iyabo to reunite under one roof.

Therefore, as a result of rescue mission 4, Sunny ended up living with his aunt once again. But the promise to put Sunny in a primary school was broken for a while. Rather than put him into school straightaway, he was used like a houseboy, doing all kinds of family chores. He could not go to bed until everyone else had gone to bed. He had to sleep on the mat in the passage while everyone else slept in the bedroom. On some occasions, he might use discarded cement papers as his mattress because there were no bed or mats to sleep on. He was always the last to go to sleep and the first to wake up in the morning. This despite Sunny's dad sending a monthly maintenance allowance to his older sister to look after his two children, Iyabo and Sunny.

This is familiar story to anyone who has ever lived in an extended family. It is similar to the story of Victoria Climbie, who died in the hands of her auntie. Except Sunny lives to tell his ugly story. Sadly, there were no effective social services mechanism in most African countries, including Nigeria, to help children in similar bondage situations. This is why Sunny became an advocate of corporate parenting for children and young people in care.

Chapter 6

AN EDUCATIONAL SECOND CHANCE

Sunny was taken to the IMG Primary School following his auntie's previous registration to start his primary school. But he was now thirteen years old by the time he started in September of that year.

At first, the IMG school management refused to take Sunny. They rightly believed he was overaged for primary school and should, therefore, consider adult education. Another reason was that the school management believed that Sunny's age could create problems for the younger classmates which might lead to regular conflicts, fighting, and possible bullying. Mrs Kujore, a family friend and teacher at the school, saved the day for Sunny's education and his future. She knew Sunny and the family well. She told the school, 'I know the family very well. Sunny is a very gentle boy, and I can assure you that he will not cause any trouble for the other kids, teachers, and the school management.'

That was how Sunny's formal educational journey started with a second chance in September 1973, when most his peers were already in year 3 or 4 of their secondary school education.

Sunny became a household name in the school and around the neighbourhood for good reasons. He was a very intelligent and hardworking student, who always exceled in his academic work. He was often first in his class and at end-of-year exams, winning numerous prizes. One year he won a prize for coming first overall in maths. He also served as class captain up to year 5, when he was not only class captain but also school janitor, a senior position usually reserved for those in year 6, the final year of their primary school education, due to his exceptionally gifted, talented, and helpful nature. In his intermediate class 3 of the six years of primary education, Sunny was successful in the national common entrance education, which would have helped him to jump the remaining three years of his primary school education and go straight to secondary school. However, his dad insisted that he fully complete his primary education before considering going on to secondary education.

In his final year in primary school, Sunny became the head boy/head prefect, games prefect and football captain. Through his leadership, the IMG Primary School excelled to the unit finals in football for the first time in school history, beating many formidable opponents along the way. He was celebrated by the school during the valedictory end-of-year event for all outgoing students by the school management.

Sunny played for the government football academy called The Greater Tomorrow. Unsurprisingly, when he first arrived in Peckham, England, in summer 1986, he quickly made friends, especially among the Black people of African Caribbean origin, who appreciated Sunny's footballing abilities to the extent that almost everyone wanted Sunny on their team. He was invited to homes for a drink afterwards. Among such good welcoming breaths on arrival were Donovan and Listowell and their respective families.

Chapter 7

GIVING SOMETHING BACK

Sunny believes in giving something back. He does not believe one should always take from society or others. One of his famous inspirational quotes is from former US president John F. Kennedy: 'Do no ask what your country can do for you, but rather ask what you can do for your country.' It is this principle and his Christian upbringing that drives Sunny's values in life. One of Sunny's inspirational Bible quotes is Ephesians 4:1–13. To paraphrase that passage, it is believed that each of us is endowed with different gifts in life, but it is up to us as individuals and as a collective to use those immeasurable gifts to the glory of God and to the benefit of humanity.

In true application of those values, and despite living in the United Kingdom since 1986, he has visited his alma mater, IMG Primary School, a few times. During one of his visits to Nigeria and the school, he noticed how dilapidated the school buildings were. Following conversations with school management, he decided to rebuild a whole block of two classrooms with an office to bring dignity and a sense of pride to the school that gave him a chance in his educational journey. It was a sense of personal pride when Sunny handed over the completed building to school management at an official event in 2010, which was witnessed by his nuclear family, associates, and friends.

In his dedication speech, Sunny recited a Yoruba native proverb that says, *'Odo ti o ba gbagbe orisun re. Gbigbe ni yio gbe'*. In other words, 'A river that forgets its source, will eventually run dry without any trace.' Sunny strongly believes that nothing he may achieve would not have been possible had IMG not given him the opportunity to have a primary education, which was the foundation to all his other educational attainments as there would not have been anything to build upon. He therefore believes that he owes all his achievements to the school, which necessitated the need to do something tangible and memorable in recognition of that privilege.

Chapter 8

COMMUNITY DEVELOPMENT

It is evident why Sunny has for decades been actively participating and contributing to community development and empowerment support initiatives in his local Southwark London Borough. Like any newcomer in an area, one is mostly preoccupied with survival during the first stage of becoming part of that community. This can last for three to five years, though for some, it might be longer. However, once one has lived in an area for 10 years or more, it is incumbent on that person to try to make the place his or her home. That is exactly what Sunny has done. According to Sunny, if one does not feel fully assimilated in that new community or home, without losing one's cultural identity, after ten to fifteen years or more, there is likely a problem with that person rather than the place. If not with the individual, it must be with both the individual concerned and the community he or she is in. He reached this conclusion because, he admits, one encounter challenges anywhere you go or live, even in one's native country. It is how one rises to the occasion and find one's place in it that determines whether one will swim or drown.

Sunny's first few years were saddled with educational and patenting challenges. As a newcomer to the United Kingdom, he did not have the right to work full time, access to public funds, or anyone to provide him with regular financial support. He had to rely on the few opportunities given to him by the Home Office to do some part-time jobs This was also coupled with becoming a husband and father at the age of twenty-eight after being joined by his fiancée, Eva, the mother of his first two sons, Jacobs and Sunny.

Sadly, the marriage did not last due to circumstances beyond the control of both Eva and Sunny. They were young, naive, inexperienced, and thousands of miles from their home and extended family network.

Chapter 9

BECOMING A SINGLE PARENT

Sunny briefly became a single parent, looking after his two boys, Jacobs and Sunny. Jacobs stayed at home with his father. His brother, Sunny, was briefly taken in to foster care in Exeter so Sunny Sr could sort himself and start getting used to being a single parent. It later became apparent that Sunny Sr would not be able to sustain the temporary arrangement, and Sunny Jr went back to his mother. Jacobs was left with Sunny for a while as the Family Division of the Royal Courts of Justice in England deliberated on the final arrangements for both boys since the parents could not agree on any reasonable arrangements.

Having to combine education, parenting, and working to earn a living can hardly leave any free time to play an active role in the affairs of one's new community. But it did not stop Sunny from getting involved. He became active in Saint Luke's Church of England Peckham Parish and his local Southampton Way Tenants and Residents Association. Both allowed him to contribute positively to community cohesion.

Chapter 10

EDUCATION

Discussed in a previous chapter was how Sunny's education was hindered by the break-up of his family when he was about four years old. He did not finish his primary school education until the age of twenty. Most people of his age had already finished or about to finish their university educations.

However, while in his class 3, intermediate class, he moved back to his dad, who then lived in Ring Road Quarters Suburb. He had been living with his aunt Iya Eleko, who lived in Oke Ado, all in Ibadan. The road was not always smooth for Sunny. But he has always found a rescuer. Interestingly, most often women.

On completing his primary education, Sunny was admitted to the Methodist High School, Ibadan-Lagos Express Way, where he would complete his GCE Ordinary Level certificate. But he did not have his English certificate, despite doing very well in other subjects, even earning distinctions in some of them. So he was not able to enter university straightaway. He retook some of his papers in 1985 to enable him to enter a university degree programme.

Sunny was determined to improve his knowledge and educational attainment by enrolling with the Institute of Marketing (now called the Chartered Institute of Marketing) based in England. Nevertheless, prior coming to the United Kingdom after his primary education, he started working as a sales representative for the African Press Limited, a sister company of the *Nigerian Tribune*. It was his godmother, Mrs Omotola Oyediran's, family business. He did this for about three years, until 1986, when his best friend, Jimmy Aliu, encouraged him to come the United Kingdom with him. Sadly, Jimmy ended up in Germany a few years after Sunny had settled in England.

Let's look back. When Sunny was now twelve years old. Another year and a bit went by, and Sunny was still not in any school. And now a teenager, enrolling in primary school enrolment was becoming increasingly difficult.

Sunny was registered in St Stephen's Primary School Nalende when he arrived from his grandad's home. But it was not long before he moved to his aunt Iya Eleko's. This back and forth led to unexpected delays in starting his primary education.

Chapter 11

THE ABUSE

As mentioned previously, his aunt Iya Eleko used him like a slave when Sunny lived with her. Sadly, that is the only way he could describe it. He had to work all day, while her children were allowed to play. Sometimes he managed to sneak out to play with his friends just for a while without jumping from one finished chore to starting another. But when caught, he was scolded or even beaten with sticks or belts. The worst punishments came from Iya Eleko's older son, Sunny's uncle Oluwole.

Sunny's sister Iyabo had also practically become a slave to the family. Iyabo was also denied an education. She was used as a domestic servant to middle-class families. The worst part was that she was never allowed to keep her salaries or tips from her bosses.

When their dad became increasingly concerned about the welfare of his children and how his sister was treating them, he was reminded that a girl's upbringing was the sole responsible of another woman. Therefore, he was powerless to intervene. Sadly, Sunny and Iyabo's mother, Mariam, had remarried and divorced a few times, and had additional children to look after. So even if she were interested in the welfare of her children from her previous marriage, she had little time to intervene.

It was always a special treat for Sunny and Iyabo to see their mum once in every few years. On some occasions, Sunny had to pester his sister a bit so that a visit to their mum could be arranged. It was never because she was prevented from seeing her children or that her children did not want to see her. Perhaps she had too much on her plate. On one occasion when it was arranged for Sunny and Iyabo to visit their mum, Sunny had to be begged to return home. He did not want to leave his mum again.

Chapter 12

EARLY AMERICAN INFLUENCE

On moving to live with his dad, Sunny discovered that his dad could no longer continue his building construction contracting work anymore, even after his sight returned. However, he still suffered partial sight impairment that affected his ability to work in the construction industry. It was because of this that Sunny's dad decided to move into the security sector, which led him to working with the American consulate, then in Ibadan, guarding their homes.

As an unmarried man and a single parent with no extended family or friends support network in the vicinity, he had no choice but to risk taking Sunny to work with him at night as he did not want to leave Sunny on his own.

This went on for a few years. One night, Mr Schmidt, one of the American expatriates, saw Sunny and his dad in the outside passage corridor, trying to hide from the rain. He called Sunny into one of the duplexes to sleep, providing them with quilts, blankets, and a mattress. The bond between father and son started to strengthen. They later moved into the boys' quarters, which was now empty. Ironically, the family home was just in Ibadan, just about a thirty-minute drive away. But Sunny's dad was determined to start a new life and leave everything behind.

An American couple, Mr and Mrs Hills, had a son, Aaron, and he and Sunny became good friends by playing football and baseball together. The Hills family was able to impart some American cultural values on Sunny, which eventually shaped his life and perspectives of the world.

After the family went back to the United States, Sunny developed a relationship with the new occupants. Sunny would be asked to babysit for some of their friends whenever they had to go a dinner party. He would be asked to help with the dishes and to buying some groceries for them. These tasks provided some useful pocket money.

Chapter 13

MOTHER LOVE (GODPARENTS)

Sunny was thrown back and forward most of his life, until 1977/1978, when his life was about to change for the better. He had just returned to his dad, Jacob Lambe Sr, who was working for the American consulate as a security officer for one of their residential homes in Ring Road, opposite Oyediran's (Professor and Mrs Oyediran, Pa Obafemi Awolo's daughter) family house. His love for young people was about to pay off. Sunny would bring some of the local young people around to play with Aaron Hills and his sister, the two young children of Dr and Mrs Hills. They were about five and seven years old. They would all play together, and through this, Olumide Oyediran was invited to play football with them in the large compound. This relationship developed into Olumide adopting Sunny as a big brother, leading to Sunny's introduction to the mother, Mrs Omotola Oyediran, who would later become Sunny's godmother. Sunny spent more time with the new surrogate family than with his own biological extended family. The Oyediran family—Chief Mrs Oyediran, Professor Oyediran, and the whole family—looked at Sunny as one of their own. He had unrestricted access to their home and children, and extended family connections to the point that nobody knew Sunny was not related to the family.

At this time, Sunny was still in primary school, despite being in his teenage years, due to family dysfunctionality. However, his newly found family afforded him the opportunity to learn from middle-class and upper-class children. He received help with his homework on tricky subjects from Yewande Oyediran (now Mrs Subir), Ayotola Oyediran (Mrs Ayodeji) and Dolapo Soyode (now Dolapo Osinbajo, wife of the vice president of Nigeria). These women became sources of inspiration and hope for Sunny, including the motivation to continue his education until his primary school in 1979.

Chapter 14

BULLYING

You never know how much damage bullying does to the confidence and self-esteem of the victim until one is a victim himself or herself. As if growing up with a single-parent dad and all the uncertainties that come with that were not enough, being bullied by your playmates and trusted extended family members was another. Among some of the most important needs on Abraham Maslow's hierarchy of needs is the need to belong. We all want to belong, feel loved, and be accepted by our families, friends, and loved ones. In some desperate situations, we may do anything to feel loved and wanted. Sunny was no exception. Having lost his mother's love and care at the tender age of about three, it was not surprising that he trusted almost anyone who showed him at least a little bit of love. Sadly, that could also be catastrophic to a child's development.

Sunny used to be bullied and cheated by his playmates, most of them living with both parents. In order to feel a sense of belonging and fill the emptiness in his life, Sunny would hand the boys his pocket money just to feel a bit of the love which was missing in his life. Sometimes friends and their families tend to be understanding and welcoming, while others used to humiliate and abuse Sunny physically, mentally, and emotionally, making him even more like an outsider.

On one occasion, Sunny and his playmates went to the stream to catch fish. They managed to catch a few. Tunji, his playmate and supposedly best friend, caught some fish. Sunny naively thought he and Tunji were best of mates as they hung out together a lot. On returning to town with their catches, Tunji joined another group, who happened to be his real friends. When Sunny asked for his share of the fish, they all descended on Sunny and started beating him. That was D-Day. A new Sunny—confident, outspoken, and with a no-nonsense attitude—came out of his shell. He stood up to the bullies, who always took his pocket money and pushed him around. He rose up against the bullies and saved the day. The bullies ended up becoming his friends when they realised the new bold and confident Sunny was willing to fight for fairness and equality. Throughout Sunny's childhood, it became the norm for Sunny to defend anyone he found being cheated, abused, or taken advantage of by individuals or corporate bodies. Sunny used to get into a lot of trouble just because he was fighting for others.

Chapter 15

DEAL OR NO DEAL

Apprenticeship or Further Education?

Sunny received an admission at one of the best secondary schools, Methodist High School, Ibadan to start Form 1. However, looking at his age of now 20-year-old, Sunny's dad, suggested that he should consider applying for a vocational skill apprenticeship of some kind. It came like a sharp knife stab in Sunny's heart when he heard that. He was sad, confused and disorientated. At first, he did not know what to do. His dreams and aspirations in life are now crumbling in front him. As young as Olumide Oyediran was at that time, despite the huge age differences of more than nine years, there was so much true brotherly love between both of them. They had forged a strong brotherly bond together. Olumide said to Sunny, *'Why not speak to mum about your predicament?'* Sunny was very shy and reluctant to ask for somebody's parent for help that his own parents would not be readily giving. Therefore, Olumide led the way and asked his mum, now late Chief Mrs Omotola Oyediran, for help on behalf of Sunny. Mrs Oyediran, commonly called 'mummy Ibadan', said abruptly,

'Why can't he ask me himself? Who is older between both of you? Sunny's godmother said, sarcastically. Then Olumide said, you know bra Sunday is very shy. Then mummy said, okay we are going to the Methodist High School on Monday to pay your school fees and arrange for anything else you may require for start school. That was the end of the story. So, the following Monday, Mrs Oyediran got Sunny in her Mercedes Benz Car, and off they went to pay for his school fees. When she was asked about the relationship between Sunny and herself. She said, 'My son'.

Mother's love

Late Chief Mrs Omotola Oyediran was a great godmother and political influence in Sunny's life. They became inseparable, going everywhere together, including political campaign rallies. It was often said in Yoruba that, 'bi igbin ba fa, ikarahun a tele'. If one sees a snail, it's shell is never far behind. So, wherever one sees mama, Sunny is never too far away from there as well.

Sadly, Chief Mrs Oyediran, Sunny's godmother died peacefully at home in 2020. She is survived by Prof Olukayode Oyediran her husband, who has also been a great godfather, role model on moral, academic, intellectual and professional development influences in Sunny's life and career development. All these were complemented by love and support from Kemi, Yemisi (Yewande), Ayotola and Olumide. Same love were also extended to Sunny from Segun Awolowo, Funke Awolowo and Dolapo Soyode (Dolapo Oshibajo, wife of Nigeria Vice President). The story won't be complete without mentioning Yemisi Balogun (Mrs Ogunba), who was Papa Awolowo's niece. There are other friends who were of great influence in Sunny's life as well such as the Morenikeji family, most especially Dr Deji Morenikeji who would help Sunny with his science subjects, despite the age differences.

Living with an Alcoholic

The worse thing is not knowing that you are an alcoholic. This was the story with Sunny's dad, Jacob Lambe snr. He never married again since the breakup of his first marriage to his childhood love, Mariam,

Sunny's mum. Nobody knew that he never recovered from it. He would spend most his time in the beer parlours until his monthly salaries ran out. Sunny became the carer instead of the cared for. Sunny had to learn to be independent very quickly, including cooking and washing for himself as dad may not return home until late in the night or the following early morning. Sometimes, with bruises on his face and body received from falling into gutters. On one occasion, Sunny's dad had a few drinks before he went to work while guarding the Americans. His boss discovered that he was drunk. Therefore, he was now steering a sack in the face. As soon as he realized what was about to happen to him and his son-possible loss of his job and the free accommodation, he became sober very quickly and decided to use Sunny's social capital with the American bosses to regain his job. In the middle of the night, they both went to Jacob's employers. On seeing Sunny, they let them in. Sunny begged them on behalf of his dad. That was how Sunny's dad was reinstated back into his job and was allowed to keep all his privileges as well.

One another night Sunny and his dad were returning home from one of his dad's binge drinking with friend. Dad carried him on his back while Sunny was holding tight to dad's neck. It was raining heavily with slippery floors. Sunny's dad lost his balance and they both fell into a shallow gutter. They both pick themselves up and went home. Both Steptoe and son were inseparable. Sunny's dad would do anything to protect his son. The fatherly bond was very strong until the day he died.

Amazing Grace!

Stealing doesn't pay! Any child growing up with a single parent is more vulnerable than a child growing up in a two parents background with extended family network support. It was even more difficult for a single dad those days because divorce was not common in the sixties and seventies. Secondly because most men were not prepared for single parenthood, both mentally and physically. However, trusting friends and neighbourhood support networks for that extra support was common to both gender single parents. Therefore, whilst that sense of village parenting was the norm, the care, love and attention from own biological parents can never be underestimated. Furthermore, as a single parent, one cannot be able to provide everything the child needs. Sunny's situation was not an exemption. On this particular occasion. Sunny had asked his dad to buy him a pair of trainers like all his peer group they played together. Dad promised to buy it as soon as money came to hand. One day, Sunny went to the local primary school football playground to play football with his friends. Usually, all kids had to take-off their trainers when playing or if you are lucky to have two, one puts the second pair on the side of the goal.

This gave Sunny the opportunity to help himself with a pair of trainers that belonged to somebody else, now lying around. He took the trainers and went home. He knew his dad would be extremely mad with him if he finds out, so he hide it in a pillow case somewhere at home in the bedsit he and his dad were sharing.

After play, owner of the trainers was looking for it. On investigation, one of the other kids suggested it might be Sunny who took it. Therefore, they went to Sunny's house in the night. They met Sunny's dad at the door. Dad asked if Sunny took the trainers. He denied any knowledge of it. Dad asked him again, he denied flatly. Sunny's dad went inside the house to search everywhere. He found the trainers, returned it to the owner and apologized the young man. Sunny's dad looked at him disappointingly but he did not do anything at that point. He waited a few days after Sunny had forgotten all about the incident. As he was going to work that particular morning. He woke Sunny up for a chat about the previous night incident. He took out his belt and beat the living daylight out of him. Later, he started crying. Sunny then asked why. He said, 'I was not happy smacking you. However, stealing is not good. It can only bring shame and dishonour to you and your loved ones. Work hard and be content with whatever you can afford in life'. He further said to Sunny. There is money and fame, including death and prison. Make your choice. However, you can wait long enough and work hard, you can achieve anything you put your mind to in life. This was one of the first practical moral lessons Sunny's dad taught him. It put him in the straight and narrow and whenever the going gets very tough and about to get tempted, this lesson always served as a great deterrent. Sunny also recalled the message his dad always sent him through his letters when he first arrived in England in the late '80s; which always says; 'Remember the son of whom you are'. It was a common phrase used in Yoruba culture to educate and warn a child not to bring shame and dishonour to the family by soiling their family name in search of money and fame at all cost.

It Wasn't Me

One of the disadvantages of living with extended families apart from the loss of love, care and attention from one's natural parents was the fact that one would always get blamed for everything that may happen in the family. If milk runs out in the fridge, it must the outcast that finished it and failed to raise alarm for a replacement. If a window is broken, it would be blamed on the outsider living with the family. If money is stolen and or a piggy bank is broken with monies inside taken away, it would be blamed on that child. If one denies doing, one is branded a liar even if it is true that one did not do it. That was the experience of most outsiders and a fostered child, formal or informal.

Therefore, that was the experience of Sunny as he was always blamed for everything he did not do but happened in his aunt's house. Even if he denied doing it, they would still blame it on him and call him a liar.

Children used to be encouraged to save their pennies, loose change and pockets monies. Each child would be bought a clay bank.

Somebody has been breaking into the children's piggybanks in the house and taking all the money in it. Sunny was accused of breaking the piggybanks and taking all the money in them. So, because he was always blame for every horrible things that happened in the family, so it was not surprising that he was the first person that was accused of taking the money. Since Sunny was always blamed for similar incidents in the past without any evidence. So, said he did break the banks when it was not even him.

Therefore, Sunny was given a few lashes of kobobo as the alleged confessed thief in the family. He now has to take everything coming to him for future deterrence.

As his aunt had already given Sunny a little chastisement, for the wrongful offence. Sunny's uncle Wole became remorseful and confessed that he was the one that was always taking all the piggybank monies whenever he was broke. Sadly, his mum, just laughed it off as if it was nothing without considering the emotional and psychological effect on Sunny who was constantly blamed for stealing he never did. That was the day Sunny made himself a promise that no matter what, he would never confess to a crime he did not commit in future. Therefore, that was the beginning of another episode in Sunny's life.

A Dream for My Sister

Sunny had wanted to study printing having observed one of his uncles who was a typesetter. Sunny was vaccinated by it. He received the deadliest blow of his life when his uncle categorically told him that he could never become a printer or work in a printing press unless he could read and write. It was because of the realization that without literacy he could never enrol on the printing course that led Sunny's determination to go back to school at the age of thirteen. Sunny later worked at his godmother's printing press company as a sales representative and production executive before coming to England.

Without Iyabo, Sunny's older sister's intervention, Sunny would not have had any primary certificated education in life, despite dad's efforts to provide him with some private tuitions at the earlier stages of his life. Both Iyabo and Sunny were living with their aunt, their dad's older sister in an informal foster parenting relationship, which was very common within the Yoruba communities and other cultures in Africa. At this time, Sunny had left to live with his aunt, who was also a single parent with five children of her own, with the oldest already married. Mama Eleko would use Sunny and Iyabo, his sister to do all the odd jobs and chores in the house, waking them up as early as 5am. Mama Eleko did not put Iyabo into any formal school education neither did any of her three other daughters, except the two boys, second and last born children who happened to be boys. That was the case for women. Sadly, not much importance was given to women education in the 60s and 70s. A woman would rather be encouraged to go and learn some practical vocational skills or trade such as tailoring/sewing, retailing, artisan skills etc. rather than been put in a formal education. It was believed that she would soon move to her husband and start rearing babies. That was their thinking. So, Iyabo, was directed into becoming a housemaid following becoming a teenager. She was never encouraged to go to school.

Therefore, now Sunny joins his older sister, Iyabo, living together with their foster parent and auntie. The auntie kept using both of them to look after her own children and grandchildren as errand boy and girl, including using them as cashcows to make money to look after her own children.

Meanwhile, Sunny's dad is now very crossed with his sister for the way her sister was treating his children. He threatened to come back for Sunny, as custom would not allow him to take his daughter from the sister. Now

Iyabo, Sunny's older sister became bold and demanded from their aunt, that Sunny should be allowed to go to school, as they had already denied her the same opportunity. She insisted that her brother, Sunny must be given the opportunity they denied her. Having an education was a dream for my sister, despite being denied the same. The aunt refused to pay for Sunny's schools fees and uniform. Iyabo had to dig out from her savings, which she was not allowed to have, since all her salaries and tips were taken by their aunt to pay bills. Sunny's educational attainments became a dream for the sister-Iyabo. The primary education became the ultimate foundation to all Sunny's educational attainments. It is therefore no wonder why Sunny believes that he owes all his life achievements to the women (sister, godmothers, wife and all women friends who have ever played any role at every stages of his life.

Knowing God

Sunny's spiritual development evolved through his evangelist dad, Jacob Lambe snr and his granddad, Pa Adebayo Ajadi Ogundiya-Fijabi. Sunny born on Sunday, but an atheist, since his dad was not a Christian at the time of his birth, but mum was. However, in the Yoruba traditional patriarchy, the grandparents always have the final say on those matters. Sunny's mother and her parents were Christians while the grandparents were not. However, something changed all that. Jacob, Sunny's dad became blind. He then converted into Christianity which then metamophorsised into becoming an evangelist and Shekere local musical instrument player in churches. Sunny's dad flirted with Cherubim and Seraphim, Christ Apostolic Church, etc. until he gave up on all of them due to his perception that religions had become money oriented, even as early as the 70s. However, Sunny was already exposed to Christianity by his dad while the grandad also played his role in broadening Sunny's understanding of Yoruba culture, language, tradition and religions as well. preparing him for journeys through life. On Sunny's relocation to his aunt, Iya eleko, who was a devout Christian, it became obvious for Sunny to follow in the Apostolic Faith with his aunt. This went on for numerous years until he returned to his dad, back and forward. Now with the influence of Sunny's godparents, Prof Olukayode Oyediran and Chief Mrs Omotola Oyediran, who are of the Anglican Church of England communion; in 1983, Sunny decided to get himself baptised at the Saint Anne's Church of England, Molete, Ibadan, Nigeria. This conversion might not have been unconnected with his godparents and their family, (the Oyedirans) who were also of Anglican Communion. It became easy for Sunny to continue on that journey at Saint Luke's Church of England, Peckham, following migration to the United Kingdom in 1986.

Unholy Marriage, Divorce, Children, and Second Chance

His upbringing, his father (Jacob Lambe Sr), his grandfather, and social economic factors influenced Sunny's perceptive on marriage and having children. He spent his early life with a single parent dad, who was also an orphan due to his mum's death when he was just a few days old. Lambe means, 'abiku' in Yoruba, 'Ogbanje' in Ibo for a child who has died a few times and reincarnated through the same parents or mother. Lambe or Olorunlambe or Ogunlambe also means, in god we trust. It is because the parents are not sure if that child is going to die again or stay.

Sunny's dad was such a child you died about three times before he stayed. Sadly, his mother died not long after he was born. His own older sister Iyaeleko, ended up being his surrogate mother at a tender age for both siblings. Therefore, Jacob Lambe snr had his own challenging upbringing, which he never talked about, as it was perceived that a man complaining or talking about these things are signs of weakness. Black men do not cry! What a false position to find oneself.

Sunny witnessed how difficult and challenging it was for his dad to cope as a single parent including the social, economic, physical, mental and emotional effects on himself and his father. This informed his decision not have marry early in life, nor to have children outside wedlock. He wanted a maximum of three children. Sunny married at the age 28 years old and his first son Jacobs Lambe Jnr was born just a year after his 29th birthday in England, having brought his childhood friend and fiancée to the UK in 1997, despite the challenges involved. It was his greatest joy in life and so proud that he now has what he could call a complete family of his own-wife, child and stable home for the first time in his entire life. Sadly, the fairy-tale was not meant to last as the pressures of married life, full time education, environmental influences now make the marriage impossible to cope with.

Dancing on Thin Ice

As a young, handsome and outgoing young man. Sunny was never short of girlfriends. He tend to get on better with women than his boys peer-group. Whilst Sunny saw this platonic relationship as something to celebrate without complicating with sexual intimacy, sometimes it could also lead to upset and disappointment on both sides. There were occasions when Sunny would fancy a girl, but would be afraid to tell her in order not to upset the good relationship they have until either of them sees the other going out with another opposite sex before the jealousy and upset kicks in. These are some of the examples of Sunny's childhood relationships as young man growing up. He was never ready to compromise their good relationship to the point that Sunny got the nickname 'arrangee' or 'mr fix-it' because he was also fixing his family and friends with the opposite sex. It got to a point that some girls became disappointed to the point they thought Sunny did not like women. One day, Sunny found his best friend who moved from Lagos to Ibadan while both of them were attending Methodist High School Ibadan, whom Sunny had provided free accommodation. He caught his best friend in a very compromising position with a girl Sunny thought they were an item, boyfriend and girlfriend. Sunny was extremely upset. It led to squabbles between Sunny and his friend. On asking the girlfriend, she said, 'Yes, we are friends before Tunde but you never declared to me that you really wanted me. Therefore, I thought we were just platonic friends and that was the way you wanted it. So, when your friend approached me, hence why the relationship evolved into a sexual level'. Sunny then made a promise to himself from that day that he would always let the any women he fancies know that he felt certain way more than platonic relationship with them. However, after his marriage breakup, as Sunny never wanted to upset anyone, even during his 6 years self-imposed celibacy, he did not disclose to certain women friends his sexual feelings towards them. This principle also influenced his decision to pause his initial relationship with his wife Jean in order to be 100% sure that he was ready for another longer-term relationship so that he would not disappoint either of them.

Some religious people may speak about karma, perhaps it might be the case in some situations or just a coincidence. Kate Samuel was a childhood girlfriend and soulmate. But due to a misunderstanding or another, they had a temporary breakup, according to Sunny's account. However, this was not the case with Kate who still believed that they were an item after over a year of not seeing each other again and while Sunny had already moved on and dating Eva, the mother of his first two sons, Jacobs and Sunny jnr. Sunny then moved to England and later married Eva and both of them having two kids together. Ironically, it was not until year 2020, after almost 37 years since the last time they saw each other that Kate and Sunny met again through social media that she informed Sunny on the phone that she never stopped loving him because she did not believe that they both ended the relationship properly. Over 35 years on, Sunny never believed even for a second that they still had anything left between both of them, though they made some serious life threatening mistakes together as young people and finding love for the first time, family background and upbringing circumstances a bit similar. Therefore, the social media reunion provided the opportunity to both sides to hear each other and most especially for Sunny to ask for her forgiveness. It was an opportunity to letting her know that he had moved on and happily married with no chance of ever renewing their relation. Sunny recounts how wonderful the moments they had shared together was with most of the family members, father, and godparents believing that both of them were going to get married. However, sadly, it was never meant to be.

Marriage

The marital challenges was affecting Sunny's education and ability to concentrate on his studies, to the point that at one time, one of the most brilliant students is now falling behind in his education. He was very brilliant in the classroom even to the point of helping his course mates. However, repeating the same level of performance in the final exams were the opposite. It has now got to the point that his college management started getting worried as Sunny kept failing his papers. Nobody understood what was going on in his life. The school that provides him visa and immigration stay renewal letters was now becoming increasingly concerned about Sunny's falling academic performances. He was advised by the College principal to sort himself out or he would be booted out of college because a course of 1-3 years was dragging into the 5th year making it looking suspicious of the real motive behind registering with the college in the first place. The college believed if the situation was not corrected speedily, it could have a detrimental effect on the college registration status. The stern warning and advice of the college management was followed by another one to one chat with the Director of Studies, an African of Ghanaian descent. He was equally concerned but more empathetic because he felt that something must have been going on in Sunny's life, which was affecting his academic studies. So, being an elder African from Ghana, felt at ease to have brotherly/fatherly chat with Sunny without looking too intrusive into Sunny's domestic life. The conclusion was that Sunny should carefully and critically examine all the issues that might be affecting his life and decide by himself the best way to move forward. He said, 'Sunny, you are an African like myself. We came thousands of miles away to better our lives, family and those around us. You can only do that if you try to make better your life first. Ask yourself honestly if you are in a position to do that right now. If not, then perhaps you should cut loose of anyone and anything that could be posing an obstacle in your life. A word is enough for the wise. Good luck!"

The above were the outcome of the counselling conversations between Sunny and his director of studies, which would later make a huge difference in Sunny's future, academic life and what he has become today.

Sunny had a chat with his then wife. It was not as straightforward as he had thought. He had to use a bit of cajolement, diplomacy and soft persuasion to cut himself loose.

He filed a d-i-y divorce papers for the annulment of the marriage at the family division of the Royal Courts of Justice in London. It was an involuntary breaking of promise to himself because he promised not to ever break up after marriage nor have children outside wedlock.

Divorce

Prior to the decision to file for a divorce as the last resort, he was very depressed and taking prescriptions from his local GP, not even realising that he was depressed.

On realising what was about to happen with the divorce and the future ramifications of the breakup on everyone, the divorce proceedings became more contentious and emotionally draining for all parties involved and their loved ones. It became messy and one of the most acrimonious divorces. It took weeks and months for a final resolution. Nevertheless, the immeasurable negative effects on the whole family including the two boys from the marriage would last for decades to come.

Sadly, Sunny's third promise to himself that he would only marry once in life was about to be broken just over a year of having their first son. Things started falling apart in the marriage. It became an upwards and downwards struggle a marriage. However, since both couple were still very young at the time, in their late 20s, it was felt that things would get better as time goes on. The second child was born, sadly, rather than things getting better, the relationship was getting worse each day, to the point that Sunny was contemplating returning back to Nigeria as he was no longer enjoining his marital life nor living in England. He is now about to break his third promise to himself of never to break up in marriage or have children outside wedlock.

Second Chance

The negative effect of the first marriage coupled with Sunny's childhood negative experiences of his own parents' breaking up at the age of just two years old, similar age as his first son, proved to become a deterrent to Sunny's future relationships, including contemplation of marriage.

Having had to spend some time as a single parent looking after his two boys, off and on, first son now just about 5 years old, while the second son was just about 2 years old, it was proving to be too much to swallow. He practically had no social life. He would pick up and drop his first son off at the local primary school and then drop off the younger two year old at the childminders, who were also witnesses at the court hearings for custody fights between both parents.

Sunny could hardly cope with being a full time student and single parent to young children of 2 and 5 years old. This was clearly a tall order for anyone, most especially a young man with no material or parental expertise or experience.

Following advice from a family friend, Renny, Sunny took the decision to take the younger sibling, Sunny Jnr to a foster parent in Exeter while the older brother, Jacobs was staying with him. It was still a struggle for Sunny to combine parenting and full time education together, including having to work in the post office in the evenings while the court proceedings were going on. It was not surprising that the court decided that Sunny Jr should be returned to the mother while Jacobs was allowed to stay with his dad. It remained a big struggle. Eventually, court decided to return both children to their mother who, accepted reluctantly, as was now enjoying her newly found extra freedom, which was the main cause of concern, and divorce application for unreasonable behaviour.

Starting a new life was difficult. It is now sixth years on when since the divorce in 1992. Sunny was reluctant to engage in any serious relationship because of fear of another failure. Now to make matters, he has now completed his first degree and an MBA while his immigration visa was now on an indefinite freeze by the Home Office, due to all the traumas of the acrimonious divorce between him and his previous wife. Sometimes when a new relationship was about to blossom into a new beginning, it always ended through suspicion from both sides. The woman might think Sunny was only interested in the relationship because of his now challenging immigration status while Sunny's reluctance was based on the feeling of 'once beaten, twice shy'.

This loneliness went on until Christmas December 1996 when Nicky, Emmanuel's wife a family friend virtually introduced Jean, Sunny's new wife to each other. It was meant to be at the Christmas party for the formal introduction to take place. Unfortunately, Jean, not that a sociable person, did not turn up at the Christmas party, even though Sunny did. Jean has had her own personal life experience of disappointment with a 7-year-old daughter, Lola, who would eventually become Sunny's daughter with much love and mutual respect between them.

At the Christmas party, two other eligible single women were introduced to Sunny. Sunny then decided to concentrate on Jean, who was absent at the Christmas party before making up his mind. In the meantime, Nikky, Jean's friend had warned Sunny, highly recommended Jean and asked Sunny to promise to treat Jean well. This gave some shockwaves into Sunny. Weeks and months went by without the expected matchmaking introduction taking place. Sunny started pestering Vikky for Jean's contact details, which went on for several weeks. Nicky eventually obliged and gave Sunny Jean's number, which started the initial direct conversation between Jean and Sunny. This went on for about 9 months, but they never met. Interestingly, love between both Sunny and Jean started growing each day that went by. On realising this and the fact that Nikky had already warned Sunny about not trying to play any silly games if he was not ready for a new serious relationship. This forewarning gave Sunny something to consider very carefully and ask himself if he had recovered the earlier breaking up of his first marriage and was ready to start afresh.

Sunny decided to put a temporary freeze on the new virtual relationship for a few months, which lasted several months. It was exactly about 7 months of no telephone conversations, no physical, pictorial or video recognition of each other when it dawned on Sunny that he actually love Jean, ready to move on, and then decided to contact Jean again. At first, he was reluctant because over 7 months has passed since he last spoke Jean and Lola her daughter. Sunny was afraid to intrude if she had already moved on and started a new relationship. Therefore, he was very reluctant to contact Jean.

Sunny eventually summed up the courage and called Jean. It was Lola, who would eventually become Sunny's daughter (stepdaughter) who was first to the phone. On hearing Sunny' unique African accent from the other end of the landline phone, she said, 'Hello Sunny' as she used to referred to him at the time. After a few minutes pleasantries, Lola said, 'Let me call my mum for you'. Sunny's greatest weakness was forgetting people's names; ironically, he was able to remember Lola's name straightaway. That spelt the beginning of a new relationship and a second chance and the solemnisation of that new beginning since 4 July 1998 and since blessed with two additional siblings to Lola- Shona and Aaron Lambe, respectively. Who says there are no second chances in life! It was a most memorable day with Sunny and his best man, Martin French signing the witness register. The story may not be complete without mentioning Richard Timmis, Sunny's solicitor friend who was always there to support him during the most challenging time fighting his time to remain in the UK.

Coming to England

Sunny never wanted to travel out of Nigeria. He did not really like flying, saying goodbyes nor leaving any area that he feels comfortable and already made a home and become part of, even if it becomes uncomfortable and challenging later. He always tries to become part of the solution to any problems that might evolve, no matter where from and how challenging it might be. Perhaps it might be attributed to his challenging upcoming and family dysfunctionality at the early stages of his life. While progressive in outlook, he also shares some traits of a conservative even though he describes his political views as progressive liberal and social democratic. However, these traits are evident by his ability to work with all main UK major political parties, despite being a member of and Labour Party elected councillor; having served in the capacities of both the Secretary General and Chairman of the Association of British Nigerian Councillors UK for a while.

The idea of coming to the United Kingdom could be credited to his best friend, Jimmy Aliu, who put the idea into his head. Everything happened so fast that even the host family in the UK, Lanre Bankole and his wife who welcomed Sunny until he was able to stand on his own two feet. Sunny came in with his Nigerian green passport fresh from the production line without requiring any visas for entry as a Commonwealth citizen. The Commonwealth citizenship allowed citizens of former British colonies to enter Britain without any need for prearranged visas. It also allowed one to change his/her immigration entry status from visitor to a longer stay including becoming a student if one so wishes, an opportunity which Sunny took advantage of to improve his life.

A month entry visa has now turned into over 35 years following entry in 1986 with UK now become the first home. Thanks to the Bankole family who offered him home before soldering on and Michael Jacques, who offered him his first job as a painter in a local fitness club. Sunny's story would not be complete without mentioning some great friends he was fortunate to have met along the way such as Jacob Abe and Sokari Douglas Camp CBE who became sources of inspiration. Very proud to have met Sokari who has now become arguably one of the most famous African sculptors, including being a woman, in the world with her creative artistic cultural exhibits being celebrated, admired and showcased around the world and at the Africa Centre in London.

African Voices

As Sunny became grown, enlightened and more socially aware of the society, world affairs and the unequal world, he became interested in world current affairs, the environment and equality issues. Despite his delayed education and late start in life, including financial challenges, Sunny decided to enrol for an MBA programme after his first Chartered

Institute of Marketing Diploma in Marketing Management. He went on to do his Masters in Marketing Management with his thesis on 'African Common Market by the Year 2000'. The situation became the beginning of his love for community development and empowerment including all the associated projects he founded such as the Confederation of Professional UK, Peckham Supplementary School, Black Business Initiative, Black Business Awards, Southwark Youth Enterprise Project etc. Sunny has won numerous recognition awards as a result of his immeasurable selfless positive contribution to community development and empowerment among which are Southwark Civic Award, the Honorary Liberty of the Old Metropolitan Borough of Camberwell and Southwark, Gathering of Africa's Best Award, Change Maker's Awards, and numerous other similar recognition awards.

Trade Union Movement

Sunny Lambe, Union Leader, Associate
Grades Postpersons, 1989-1994

It was autumnal December 1989 Sunny joined the Royal Mail, Post Office sorting unit as an Associate Postperson following working in the McDonald's for a while as a full time student. In January 1990, things were about to change for Sunny when his fellow part time postal workers, called Associate Postpersons unanimously agreed for him to become their representative for the first time. The part time postpersons never used to receive any unsocial hours benefits allowances whenever they were working in the evening, weekend or public holidays. It was always a single rate. This problem started when the Post Office management wanted to change the work pattern, to introduce some degree of flexibility, which met stiff opposition from the Union of Communication Workers then, now called Communications Union. The new terms of working condition was not acceptable to the union. So, by the time they came back from an industrial action, the management had already introduced some of the measures the union kicked against which was too late to overturn. This led to the emergence of Associate Grade Postpersons, in the post office, who then became the casualty of the tugs of war between the post office management, the union, and thereby denying the AG Postpersons most added employment rights as they were rightly protecting their rights, but sadly at the expense of part-timers. Therefore, a meeting of all the part time postpersons was called. At the meeting, Sunny made some remarkable comments which he himself would not remember today but inspirational in the ears of his peers, leading to him being elected unopposed by over 400 part time post persons to represent them. He was very successful in fighting improvements in working conditions of all his members, which then paved the way for the Tony Blair's Labour Government adoption of the European Employment Directives giving improved employment working conditions to the Associate Grade Postpersons and all part time workers today.

Addicted Love for Peckham

Peckham was and still like a little Lagos, or Ibadan for Sunny, where he grew up. To be precise. The night sky, the lively atmosphere, the food, the diversity and interconnectivity between people and religions. There used to be a saying that if you left Nigeria decades ago and you are looking for a lost friend or relative, just come to Peckham a few times and look round the food stores, restaurants, the churches and African-Nigerian hideouts. You will surely find the person you are looking for, if not directly but certainly through somebody who knows somebody. Peckham was more popular as a village in London than Trafalgar Square or Buckingham Palace to many people then. It makes them feel closer to home. This is the magnet that brought a significant number of Nigerians, especially of Yoruba extraction to Peckham. It was not surprising to find Sunny attracted to Peckham as well.

He has made a revolution moving homes around Peckham since first arriving in the area in July 1986. It is an area where he got married and had all his children.

Changing Peckham Perspective

Peckham had, and still has its peculiar metropolitan city challenges synonymous to any such diverse area anywhere in the world. Therefore, Peckham was not an exemption in that respect with antisocial, mugging, burglaries, rundown estate, unemployment, poverty and many more unpleasant experiences anyone could think of. All these challenges were noticeable in residents' faces, actions and the physical environment they were living.

This then led the Conservative government of the time to introduce a redevelopment programme in the area, worth billions of pound, which lasted over ten years to complete. It was dubbed the biggest regeneration programme in Europe at the time. The physical redevelopment yes, but investments in human capital and local residents around job opportunities, skills development, community and youth development and empowerment were a bit short. Therefore, it was not surprising that antisocial behaviour and youth crimes increased because of a sense of hopelessness by the people, as they felt generally left behind. Though not an excuse, but coincidentally, led to numerous youth deaths in Southwark and most especially, North Peckham estate which some of the unfortunate casualties were Shola Agoro and Damilola Taylor with the latter being the most celebrated one across the nation and internationally due to the attention it drew to Peckham.

It was because of these sad events that led to Sunny's greater interest and involvement in community development, most especially on issues affecting children and young people. Perhaps a reminder of his own challenging early upbringing in Nigeria.

In October 1998, Sunny had setup the Confederation of African Professional UK to provide an effective platform for Black people of African origin who felt marginalised, economically and socially at the time. So, following on from the unfortunate deaths of Shola Agoro, Damilola Taylor and other young people in Southwark, Sunny decided to use his professional expertise and experience, the existing platform created for adults, to setup a mixed of engagement and support activities for young people in Peckham from ages 10 to 16 years; who were still in the intermediate primary school age category, which was then extended project to the younger age group.

This was how the Peckham Supplementary School (PSS) was created in 2000. Sunny and the CAP UK management trustees, whose subcommittee became responsible for overseeing the project, with Sunny acting as the founder and principal of the supplemental school. They applied to the then grant managers but were turned down due to lack of track records of accomplishment. Sadly, expertise of the **PSS** Project Management and **CAP UK** Board were completely ignored in the grant funders' decision, which on reflection should have been taken into consideration. Of course, things have changed positively since then.

This shocking outcome meant Sunny had to fund Peckham Supplementary School himself if the project was going to start. This also meant that the project launch date had to be postponed until 30 April 2001 the following year before. This delay also ensure that the project was made accessible free of charge to all children in Peckham, across Southwark and beyond.

The local **MP**, Harriet Harman **MP**, and local councillors were very gracious to help launch the project.

The bottom line was that there were hardly any youth play areas nor encouraging activities for children and young people during the period, which was perhaps responsible for the rising youth crimes in the area and across the borough. This also gave some local political decision makers reasons to review their policies and programmes across the borough.

The **PSS** provided an after school club, teaching Black History, Maths, English, Drama, etc. to the young people with the ultimate outcomes displayed during the annual Black History Month events in October each year and thereby giving the young people a sense of safety, belonging and pride in what they do.

There was briefly a **PSS** Football Club as well until other local football clubs were supported to absorb interested young people from **PSS**.

PSS was a very successful project with 250 young people benefiting who have now grown to become parents themselves. The project later attracted funding from the **BBC** Children in Need, South East London Community Foundation, National Lottery Foundation, including eventually Southwark Council until 2008 when the project drew to a close as a result of availability of numerous new youth activities for children and young people across the borough and beyond.

Promoting Self Economic Empowerment

It was realised in 2001 that perhaps something needs to done to help parents of some of those young people who were unemployed but did not know how to explore self- employment. Therefore, year 2001 saw the emergence of Black Business Initiative (**BBI**), which was an offshoot of CAP UK. The idea was that, making noise through appealing, protesting and campaigning alone was not enough to change the mind-set of the policy makers nor improve the economic situation of the young people and their family, but to Initiative some practical self-economic empowerment support programme to help Black people. **BBI** then started networking events, business support (advice, information, guidance and mentoring) for adults, interview techniques for most especially parents and friends of **PSS** students who may be interested in setting up their own small businesses but did not know how to do it. This project was then registered as a separate legal entity of its own with the Companies House in England and Wales as a not for profit with no share capital. **BBI** then went on to introduce numerous other products and services among which were monthly networking events, annual Black Business Awards in October 2004, which has been rebranded as Achievement Recognition Awards, and now in its 18th year.

BBI was rebranded as Building Blocks Initiative (**BBI**), in order to widen the scope of its operations and appeals beyond just enterprise development and support. The annual Achievement Recognition Awards (**ARA**) still runs annually under the **BBI**.

The Confederation of African Professionals (**CAP**) **UK** where all the projects metaphorsised in October 1998 was dissolved in 2008 with the aim of streamlining activities for both reasons of easier administration and financial prudence.

Investing in Enterprising Minds

As the Peckham Supplementary School was folding up and most of the beneficiaries are now becoming adults, and in order to stem the spiral of economic despondency, it was decided that a youth self-economic empowerment initiative should be setup to replace **PSS** which led to the emergence of Southwark Youth Enterprise Project (**SYEP**) 2007 which lasted until 2011. It became so successful that it received co-founding from the then Mayor of London's London Development Agency delivery vehicle for the regional government managed by the Cross River Partnership.

An Accidental Politician

Having grown up with his godparents who were descendants of one of the arguably the greatest Nigerian politician, Chief Obafemi Awolowo, and arguably the president Nigeria never had, observing how unholy and unpleasant politics was being played. This put Sunny off politics completely. It was not however surprising that Sunny then devoted most of his life to community development and empowerment in support of others which are evident by all the projects he has been responsible for setting up. Sunny's professional life changed almost completely in 2010 when Southwark Labour came to power by beating a Tory/LibDem local coalition in the borough, which lasted from 2002 to 2010. However, it was the opposite at the national level with the Tory and LibDem elbowing out the then Labour government of Gordon Brown, which brought about the David Cameron and Nick Clegg government. However, the irony was that the austerity measures meant there had to be some hard decisions about budget cuts, which then directly affected all local governments' finances and the consequences on Sunny's BBI project delivery contracts. The contracts came to their natural end in 2011 and thereby leaving the management of BBI to fight for survival with direct effect on Sunny's personal finances as well. Ironically, despite Sunny's reluctance to get involved in politics because of his early childhood experience in Nigeria, ironically, it was his godmother, Chief Mrs Oyediran who advised and encourage him to stand for a political office in the UK. Who else could Sunny have possibly listened to other than his godmother? Sunny was selected to stand in the marginal seat of South Bermondsey Ward which was then held by the LibDems since 1982, and just 32 years prior to Sunny's election in May 2014. It is true of the saying that 'politics is a bitch'. If it was left to Sunny alone, he would not have chosen to participate in active politics let alone standing for a political office in South Bermondsey, considering his good working relationship with almost every member of all the political parties in Southwark at the time and coupled with the fact that the local LidbDem/Tory local coalition government looked after him and his business interests. Sunny's new political journey started in 2014 after winning the South Bermondsey Ward seat with his two colleagues. They won all the three seats again at the polls in 2018 for the second term with him topping the polls overall. Sunny was nominated as Labour and Cooperative prospective candidate for Bexley and Bromley London Assembly seat in 2019 but was not successful at the final candidate selection stage. Sunny is however looking forward to standing again for the third term as a Labour and Cooperative candidate for the South Bermondsey Ward in London Borough of Southwark. He is determined to explore all future political opportunities that may present themselves to him in future. After having spent over 20 years helping to develop the Nigerians in Diaspora Oranisation in the UK, Europe and around the world, and having won a Nigerian Diaspora Global Hall of Fame Award in 2018, he is extremely disillusioned about the future of Nigeria and his Yoruba extraction in it. As sad as divorce is, Sunny is now one of the proponents of peaceful separation of Yorubaland from Nigeria and making it become an independent nation. *Orisha boba le gbemi, semi bi o se bami.* As a pragmatist, it means if the marriage/amalgamation of the North and South of Nigeria since 1914 and over 60 years have not produced the desired economic and social miracle, why waste even another second to end it peacefully. Sunny hopes to be able to play an active role in the future of new Yoruba nation when it eventually materializes because he is convinced that he has so much to offer a new nation and her people, both young and old.

The Future

The future is yet for us to see. Let us celebrate today while tomorrow will take care of itself.

Conclusions

Sunny often says that whatever the mind can conceive, it can surely achieve. It is important to have a focus in life. Never allow money to become the main barrier to your achieving anything in Life-whether through earlier formative life challenges in upbringing, late start in education, owing to marriage breakup, and or other challenges in life. One can still always be in control of own destiny and the future. It is what we do with the limited opportunities that come our way that matter. Always ask yourself what you can give to make the world a better place when you leave than the one you met and not just what the world-family, friends, associates and government can do for you. *'It is always better to light a candle than whinging and cursing the god of darkness'*.

Sunny's principles in life are solidly built on aspiration, compassion, spirituality and self-belief. I can do mental attitude will get you further than your dream.

What are yours in life?

Hope you find this book a source of motivation, inspiration, and progressive path in life.

One love!

Sunny Lambe

Jacob Lambe Snr 1

Jacob Lambe Snr 2

Lambe Family Children's Picture

Prof Olukayode Oyediran, Chief Mrs Omotola
Oyediran (godparents) and Sunny Lambe

Sunny and wife Jean Galley-Lambe in Egypt

Sunny Lambe Councillor Elect 2014

Sunny Lambe in his 20s, Nigeria

Sunny receives Southwark Civic Award
Picture 13 May 2006

Sunny, IMG Pry School
Children and Teachers

Sunny Lambe - Lola's Wedding

Sunny's Graduation Picture